It's a Beautiful Day

Words and Music by Michael Bublé, Alan Chang and Amy Foster

Arranged for harp by Sylvia Woods

Two intermediate harp arrangements of this song are included in this sheet music.

The first version is for lever harps tuned to the key of C.
The second version, on page 7, is for lever harps tuned to flats.
Please choose the arrangement that has been designed for your harp, and be sure to set your sharping levers as indicated in the sentence at the top of the page.

Pedal harpists may play either version. Pedal changes are included in the music.

There is a tricky sharping lever change in each version right before measures 50 and 87. Be sure to place the chord in the right hand on the downbeat of these measures BEFORE you make the sharping lever change. That way, the ringing note that you are sharping will be muffled by your fingers, and you won't hear the noise of the lever changing the pitch.

Treble clef notes in parentheses are melody notes that are played with the left hand. They are included so you can see the flow of the melody.

It's a Beautiful Day

for pedal harps, and lever harps tuned to C

Lever harp players: set your sharping levers for the key signature, then re-set the C above middle C as a C-natural.

Sharping lever changes are indicated with diamond notes and also with octave wording.
Pedal changes are written below the bass staff.

Notes in parentheses are melody notes that are played with the left hand.

Words and Music by Michael Bublé,
Alan Chang and Amy Foster

Harp arrangement by Sylvia Woods

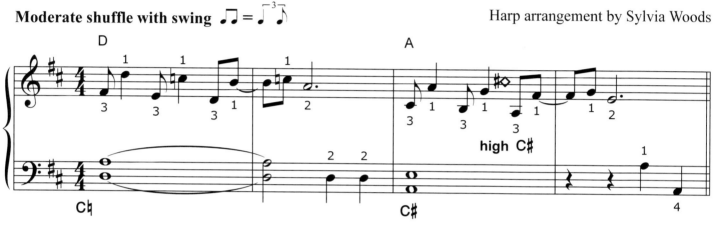

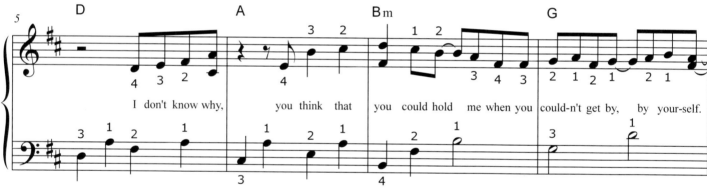

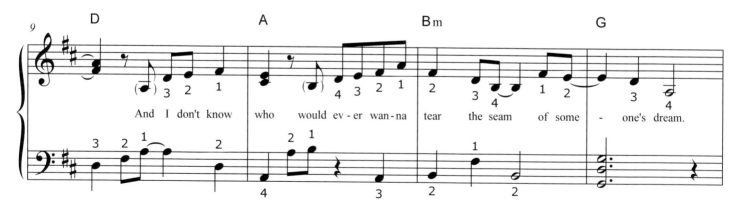

© 2013 WB MUSIC CORP., I'M THE LAST MAN STANDING MUSIC, INC., WARNER-TAMERLANE PUBLISHING CORP., IHAN ZHAN MUSIC
and SONGS FROM THE HEATLEY CLIFF   This arrangement © 2015 WB MUSIC CORP., I'M THE LAST MAN STANDING MUSIC, INC.,
WARNER-TAMERLANE PUBLISHING CORP., IHAN ZHAN MUSIC and SONGS FROM THE HEATLEY CLIFF
All Rights for I'M THE LAST MAN STANDING MUSIC, INC. Administered by WB MUSIC CORP.
All Rights for IHAN ZHAN MUSIC Administered by WARNER-TAMERLANE PUBLISHING CORP.
All Rights for SONGS FROM THE HEATLEY CLIFF Administered by SONGS OF KOBALT MUSIC PUBLISHING
All Rights Reserved   Used by Permission   Reprinted by Permission of Hal Leonard Corporation

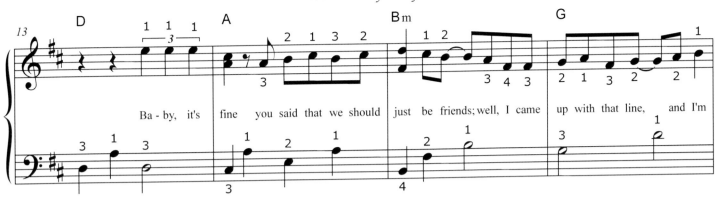

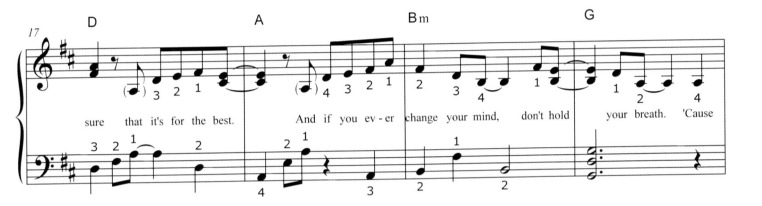

It's a Beautiful Day

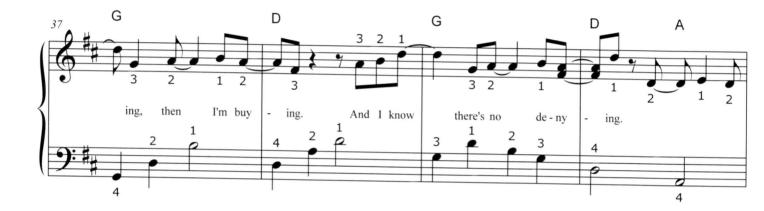

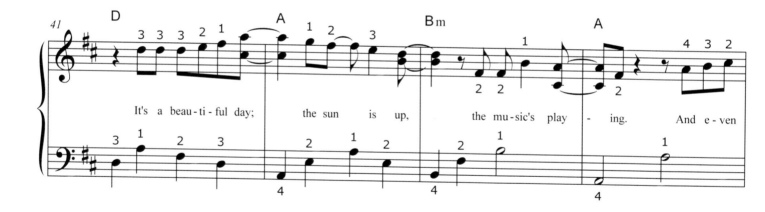

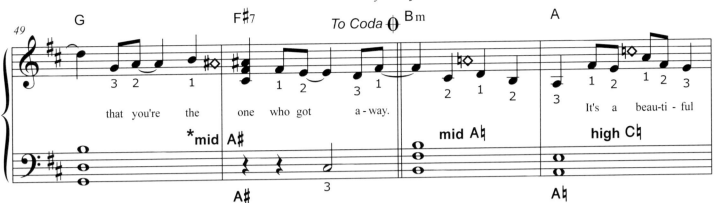

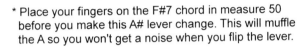

* Place your fingers on the F#7 chord in measure 50
before you make this A# lever change. This will muffle
the A so you won't get a noise when you flip the lever.

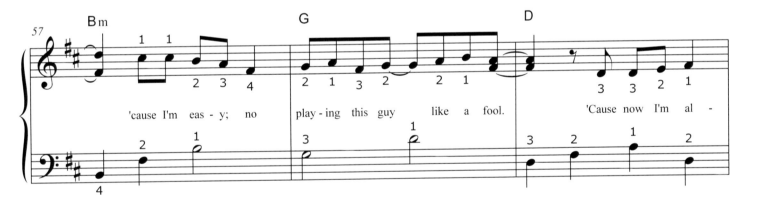

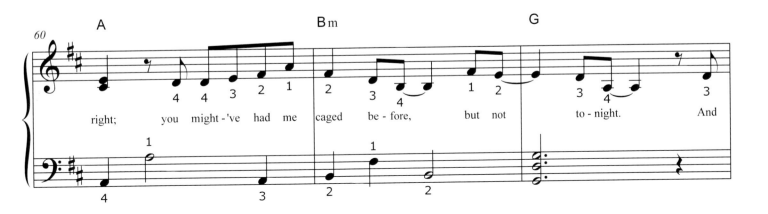

D.S. al Coda

Coda

Slower

mid A♮

'Cause if you ev - er think I'll take up my time with

think - ing of our break - up, then you've got an - oth - er thing com - ing your way.

a tempo *mid A#

* Place your fingers on the F#7 chord before you make this A# lever change.

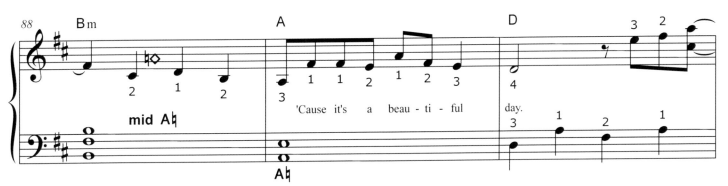

mid A♮

'Cause it's a beau - ti - ful day.

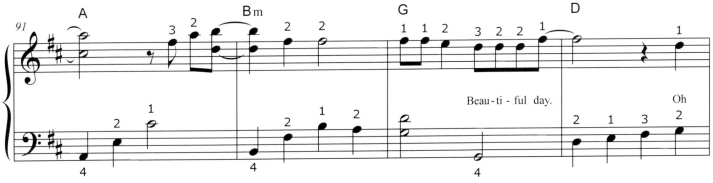

Beau - ti - ful day. Oh

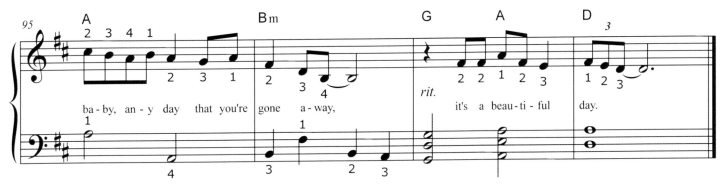

ba - by, an - y day that you're gone a - way, *rit.* it's a beau - ti - ful day.

It's a Beautiful Day

for pedal harps, and lever harps tuned to flats

Lever harp players: set your sharping levers for the key signature, then re-set the B above middle C as a B-flat.

Sharping lever changes are indicated with diamond notes and also with octave wording.
Pedal changes are written below the bass staff.

Notes in parentheses are melody notes that are played with the left hand.

Words and Music by Michael Bublé,
Alan Chang and Amy Foster

Harp arrangement by Sylvia Woods

© 2013 WB MUSIC CORP., I'M THE LAST MAN STANDING MUSIC, INC., WARNER-TAMERLANE PUBLISHING CORP., IHAN ZHAN MUSIC
and SONGS FROM THE HEATLEY CLIFF   This arrangement © 2015 WB MUSIC CORP., I'M THE LAST MAN STANDING MUSIC, INC.,
WARNER-TAMERLANE PUBLISHING CORP., IHAN ZHAN MUSIC and SONGS FROM THE HEATLEY CLIFF
All Rights for I'M THE LAST MAN STANDING MUSIC, INC. Administered by WB MUSIC CORP.
All Rights for IHAN ZHAN MUSIC Administered by WARNER-TAMERLANE PUBLISHING CORP.
All Rights for SONGS FROM THE HEATLEY CLIFF Administered by SONGS OF KOBALT MUSIC PUBLISHING
All Rights Reserved   Used by Permission   Reprinted by Permission of Hal Leonard Corporation

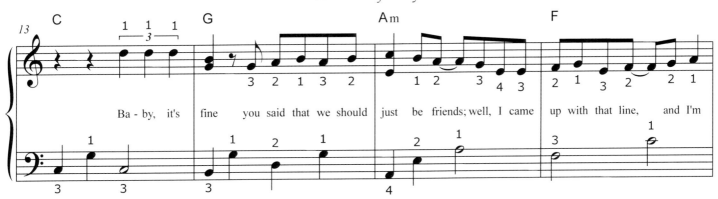

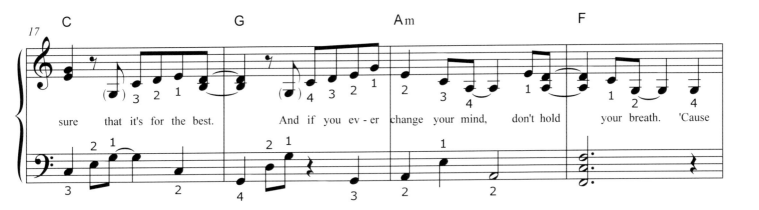

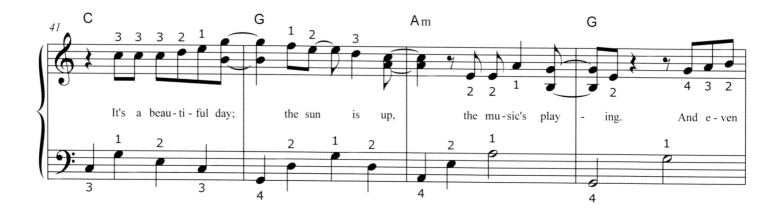

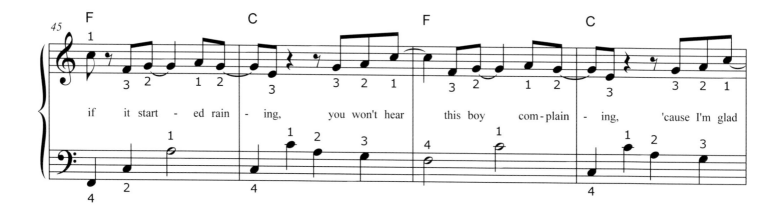

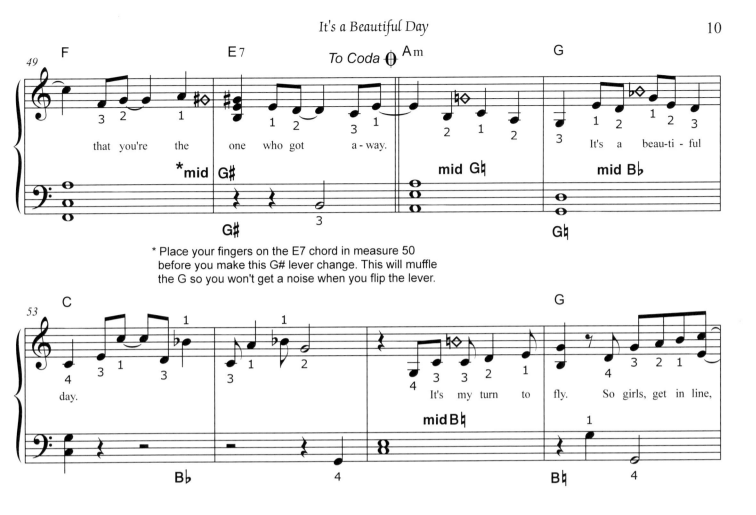

* Place your fingers on the E7 chord in measure 50 before you make this G# lever change. This will muffle the G so you won't get a noise when you flip the lever.

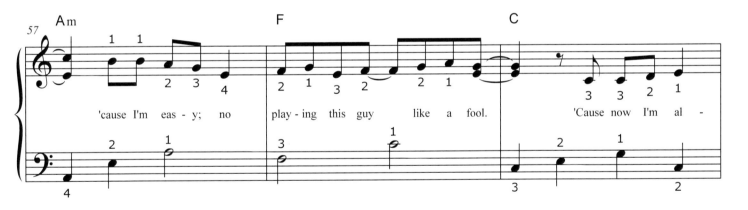

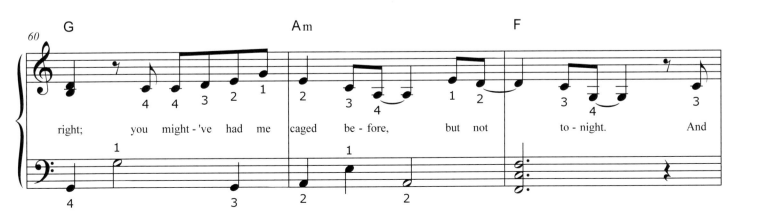

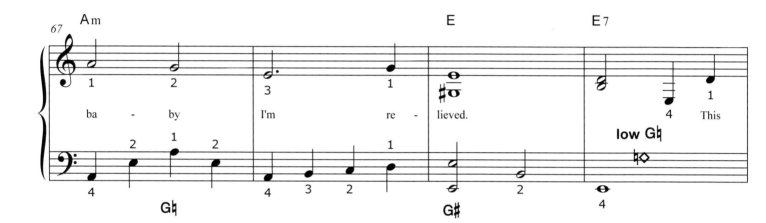

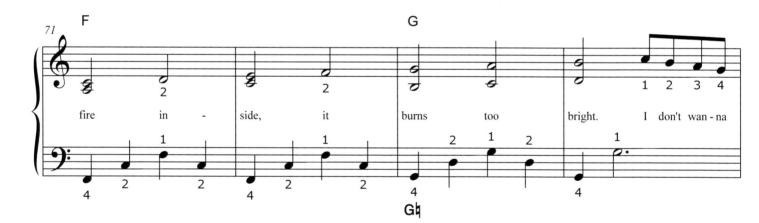

D.S. al Coda

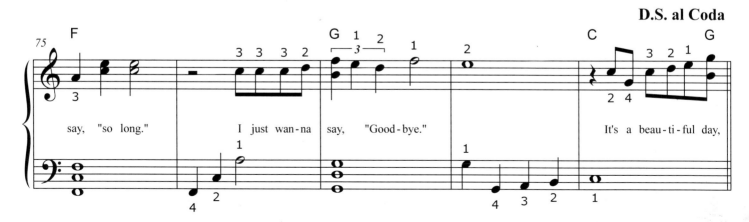

* Place your fingers on the E7 chord before you make this G# lever change.

It's a Beautiful Day

Michael Bublé is a Grammy-award-winning singer and songwriter from Canada.
"It's a Beautiful Day" is a bouncy, happy song about a romantic break-up.
It is from his 2013 album To Be Loved.

More Harp Arrangements of Pop Music
by Sylvia Woods

All of Me
Beauty and the Beast
Music from Disney-Pixar's Brave
Bring Him Home from Les Misérables
Castle on a Cloud from Les Misérables
A Charlie Brown Christmas
Dead Poets Society
John Denver Love Songs
76 Disney Songs
Everything
Fields of Gold
Fireflies
Music from Disney Frozen
Groovy Songs of the 60s
Four Holiday Favorites
Hallelujah

Happy
House at Pooh Corner
Into the West from The Lord of the Rings
Lennon and McCartney
My Heart Will Go On from Titanic
Over the Rainbow from The Wizard of Oz
River Flows in You
22 Romantic Songs
Safe & Sound
Say Something
Stairway to Heaven
Music from Disney Tangled
A Thousand Years
Andrew Lloyd Webber Music
The Wizard of Oz
Theme from Disney-Pixar's Up

Available from harp music retailers and www.harpcenter.com

ISBN 978-1-4950-4614-8

U.S. $7.95

EXCLUSIVELY DISTRIBUTED BY

HAL•LEONARD®
CORPORATION
7777 W. BLUEMOUND RD. P.O. BOX 13819
MILWAUKEE, WISCONSIN 53213

HL00150206

With many thanks to Paul Baker and Denise Grupp-Verbon

© 2015 by Sylvia Woods
Published by Woods Music & Books
P.O. Box 223434, Princeville, HI 96722, U.S.A.
www.harpcenter.com